PIANO / VOCAL / GUITAR

PENTATONIX
PTX PRESENTS: TOP POP, VOL.1

ISBN: 978-1-5400-3065-8

Visit Hal Leonard Online at
www.halleonard.com

Contact Us:
Hal Leonard
7777 West Bluemound Road
Milwaukee, WI 53213
Email: info@halleonard.com

In Europe contact:
Hal Leonard Europe Limited
Distribution Centre, Newmarket Road
Bury St Edmunds, Suffolk, IP33 3YB
Email: info@halleonardeurope.com

In Australia contact:
Hal Leonard Australia Pty. Ltd.
4 Lentara Court
Cheltenham, Victoria, 3192 Australia
Email: info@halleonard.com.au

ATTENTION

Words and Music by CHARLIE PUTH
and JACOB HINDLIN

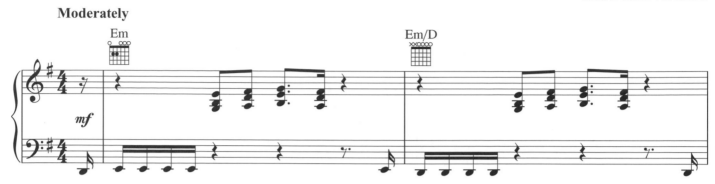

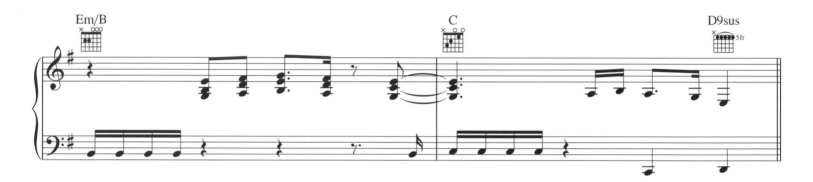

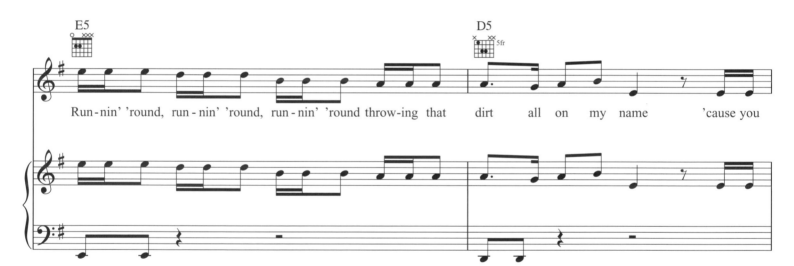

Run-nin' 'round, run-nin' 'round, run-nin' 'round throw-ing that dirt all on my name 'cause you

knew that I, knew that I'd, knew that I'd call you up, ba - by. ___ You've been

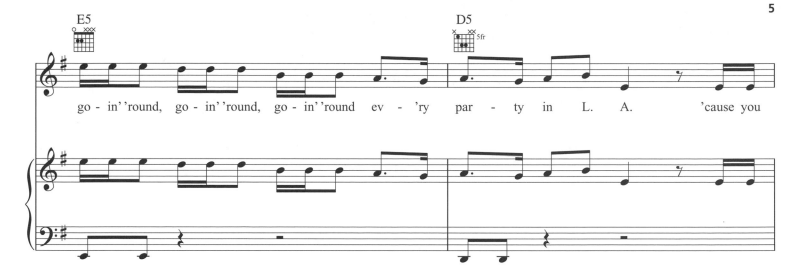

go - in' 'round, go - in' 'round, go - in' 'round ev - 'ry par - ty in L. A. 'cause you

knew that I'd, knew that I'd, knew that I'd be in one. _____

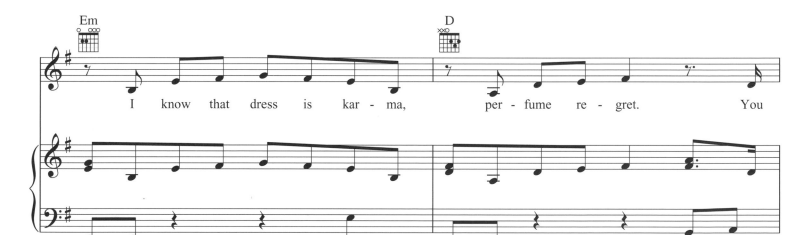

I know that dress is kar - ma, per - fume re - gret. You

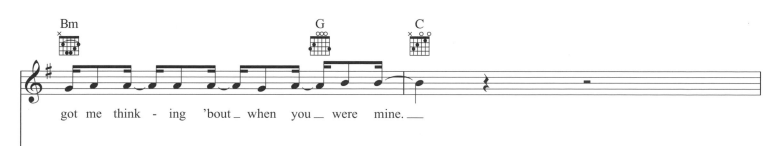

got me think - ing 'bout _ when you _ were mine. _

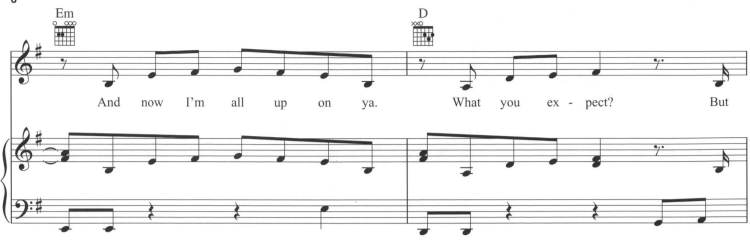

And now I'm all up on ya. What you ex - pect? But

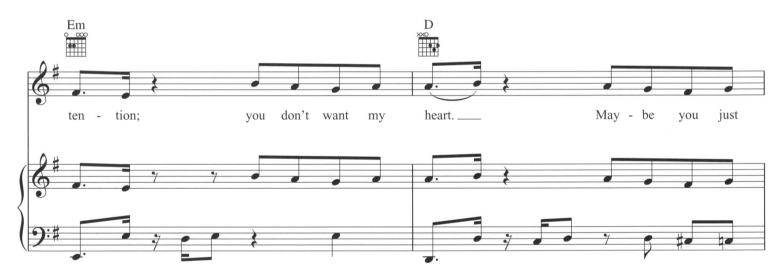

you're not com - ing home with me to - night. You just want at -

ten - tion; you don't want my heart. May - be you just

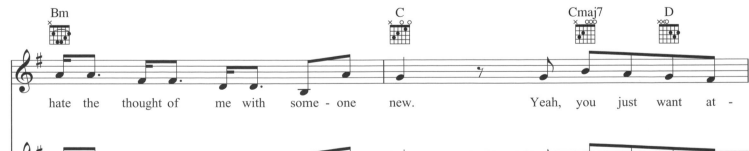

hate the thought of me with some - one new. Yeah, you just want at -

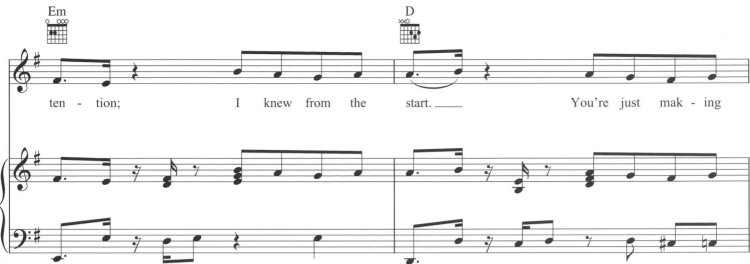

ten - tion;   I knew from the   start. ___   You're just   mak - ing

sure I'm   nev - er   get - ting   o - ver   you.

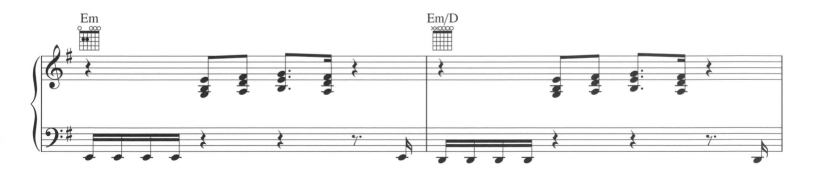

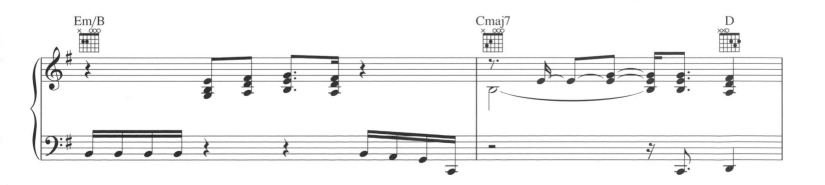

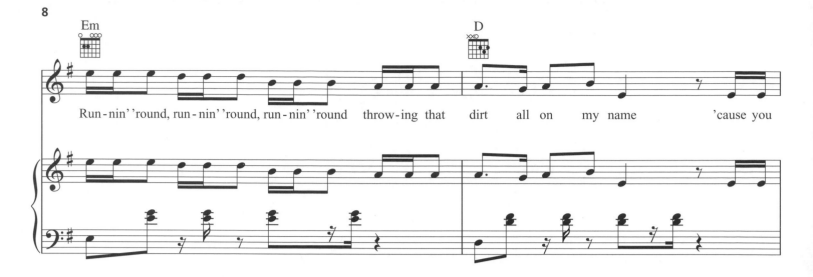

Run-nin' 'round, run-nin' 'round, run-nin' 'round throw-ing that dirt all on my name 'cause you

knew that I'd, knew that I'd, knew that I'd call you up. _____ Ba - by,

now that we're, now that we're, now that we're right here stand-ing face to face, you al-

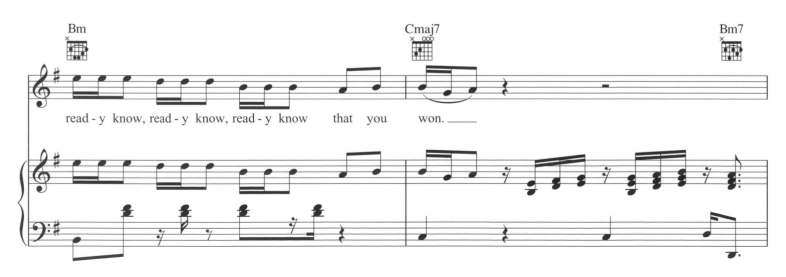

read - y know, read - y know, read - y know that you won. _____

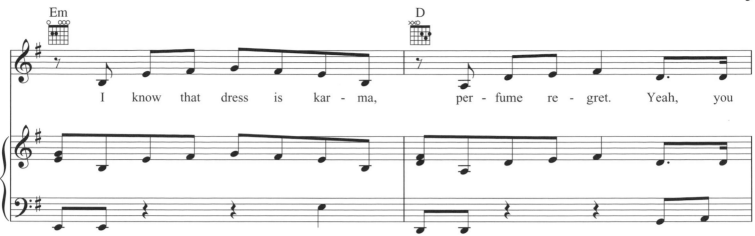

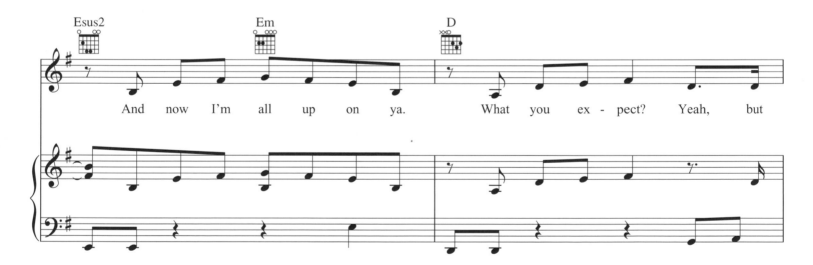

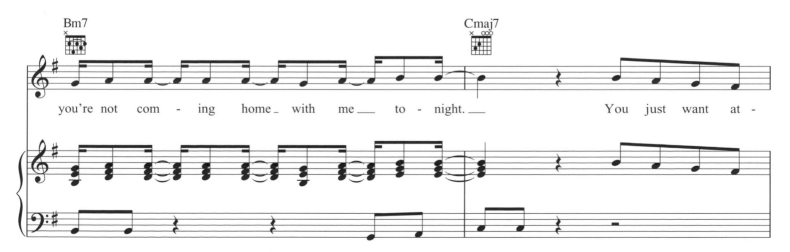

What are you do-ing to me? What are you do-ing, oh?

What are you do-ing to me? What are you do-ing? Oh.

What are you do-ing to me? What are you do-ing? Oh.

What are you do-ing? What are you do-ing? You just want at-

FINESSE

Words and Music by BRUNO MARS,
PHILIP LAWRENCE, JAMES FAUNTLEROY,
RAY CHARLES McCULLOUGH II,
CHRISTOPHER BRODY BROWN, JEREMY REEVES,
JONATHAN YIP and RAY ROMULUS

Ooh, ___ don't_ we look_ good to - geth - er? There's a rea -

- son that they watch all night long. ___

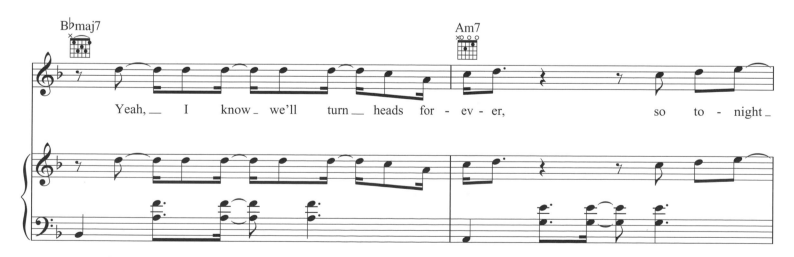

Yeah, ___ I know_ we'll turn_ heads for - ev - er, so to - night_

I'm gon - na show you off. When I'm walk - ing with

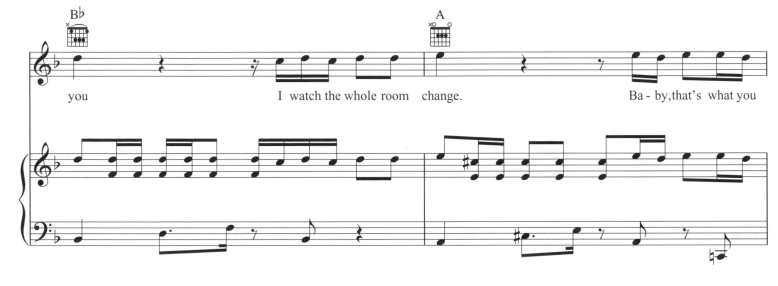

you I watch the whole room change. Ba - by, that's what you

do. No, my ba - by, don't play. Blame it on my

con - fi - dence or blame it on your meas - ure - ments.

Shut the thing down on sight. That's right, we're out here drip-ping in fi-nesse.

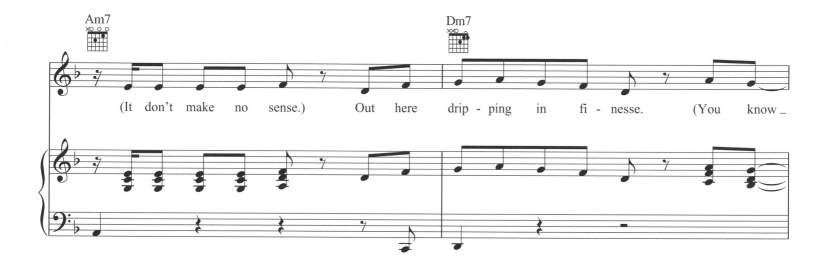

(It don't make no sense.) Out here drip-ping in fi-nesse. (You know

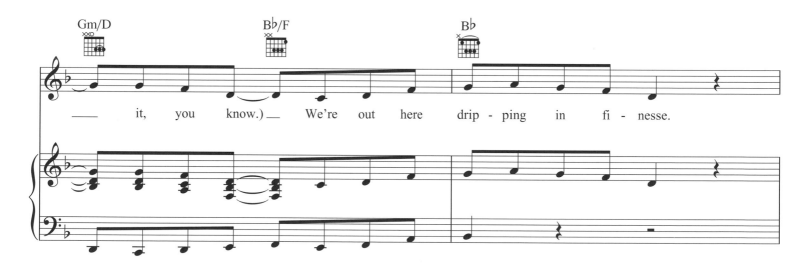

—— it, you know.)— We're out here drip-ping in fi-nesse.

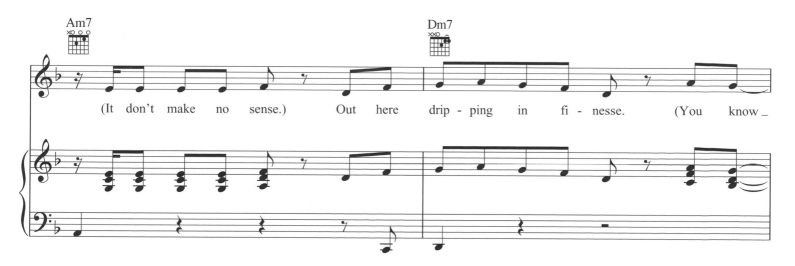

(It don't make no sense.) Out here drip-ping in fi-nesse. (You know

16

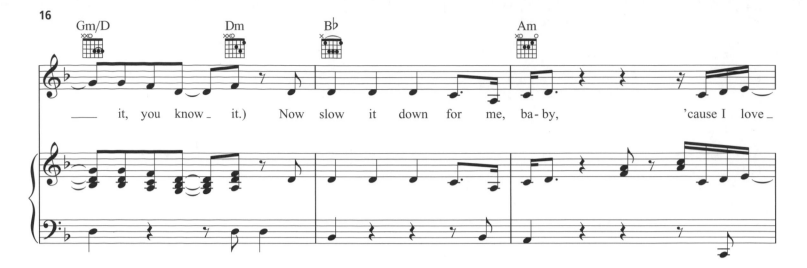

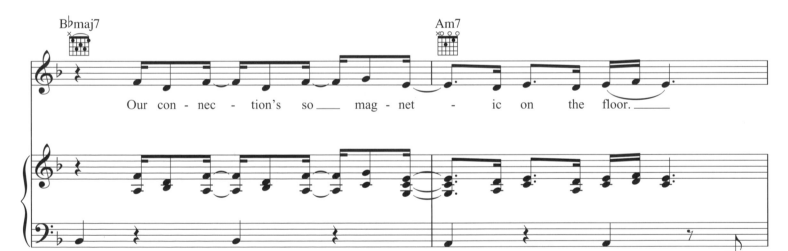

I watch the whole room change. Ba-by, that's what you

do. No, my ba-by, don't play. _____ Blame it on our

con-fi-dence or blame_ it on your meas-ure-ments. _

Shut the thing down on sight. That's right, we're out here

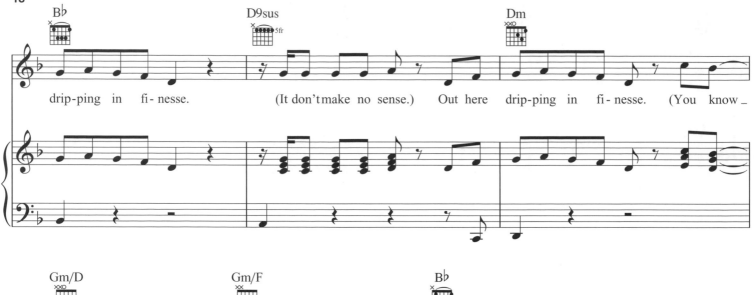

dripping in fi-nesse. (It don't make no sense.) Out here drip-ping in fi-nesse. (You know _

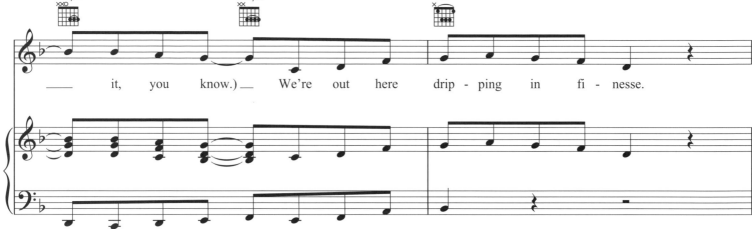

_ it, you know.) _ We're out here drip-ping in fi - nesse.

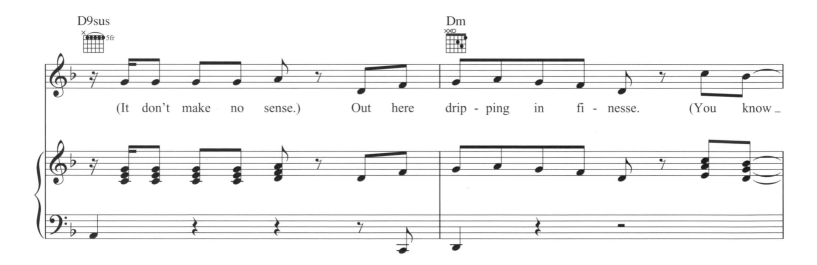

(It don't make no sense.) Out here drip-ping in fi - nesse. (You know _

_ it, you know _ it.) Fel - las, grab your la - dies if your la - dy fine.

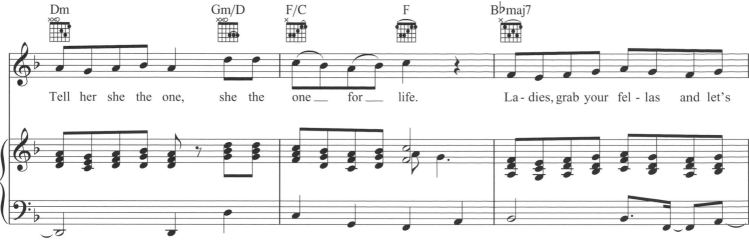

Tell her she the one, she the one ___ for ___ life. La - dies, grab your fel - las and let's

do this right ___ if you're on ___ one like me and my, (bop, bop, bop, bop). Well, we

got it go - ing on, got it go - ing on. Don't it feel so good to be us? Hey, yeah, we

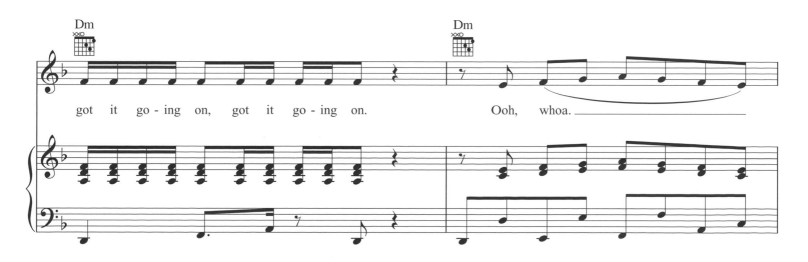

got it go - ing on, got it go - ing on. Ooh, whoa. ___

Got it go-ing on, got it go-ing on. Don't it feel so good to be us? Hey, yeah, we

got it go-ing on, got it go-ing on. Ah. We out here

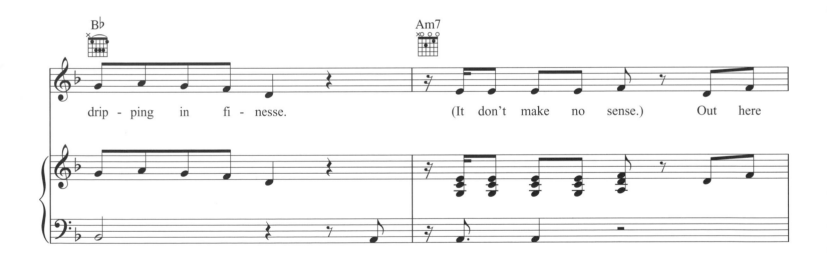

drip-ping in fi-nesse. (It don't make no sense.) Out here

drip-ping in fi-nesse. (You know ___ it, you know.) ___ We're out here

NEW RULES/
ARE YOU THAT SOMEBODY?

NEW RULES
Words and Music by CAROLINE AILIN,
IAN KIRKPATRICK and EMILY WARREN SCHWARTZ

ARE YOU THAT SOMEBODY?
from the Twentieth Century Fox Motion Picture DR. DOOLITTLE
Words and Music by TIM MOSLEY
and STEPHEN GARRETT

Moderately slow, in 2

Talk-ing in my sleep at night, mak-ing my-self cra - zy _____ (out of my mind, _

out of my mind), _ wrote it down and read it out, hop-ing it would save me.

(Too man-y times, _ too man-y times. _ My love he _

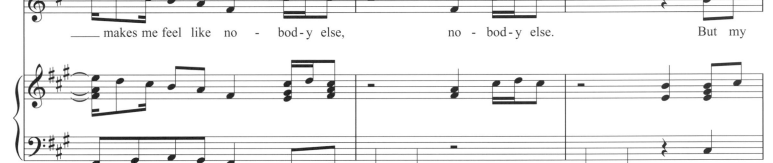

_ makes me feel like no - bod-y else, no - bod-y else. But my

love, he _ does-n't love me, so I tell my-self, I tell my-self, _

_ "One: don't pick up the phone; _ you

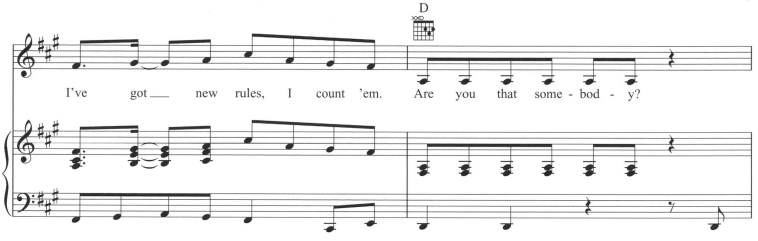

D

I've got __ new rules, I count 'em. Are you that some - bod - y?

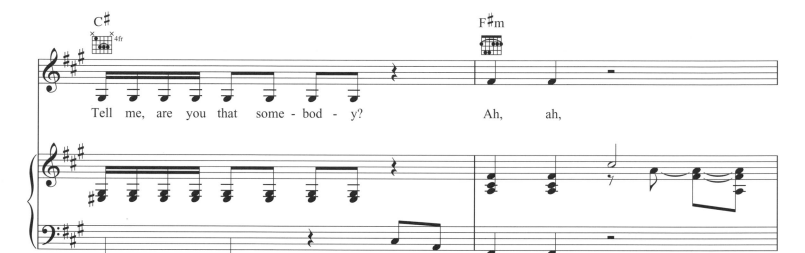

C# **F#m**

Tell me, are you that some - bod - y? Ah, ah,

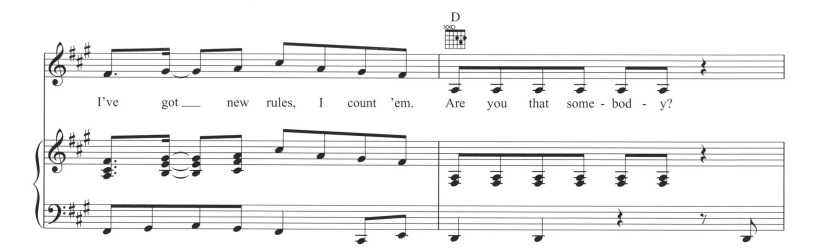

D

I've got __ new rules, I count 'em. Are you that some - bod - y?

F#m/C# **To Coda** ⊕ **F#m** **E**

N.C.

I've got - ta tell them to my - self. I keep push - ing for - wards but he keeps pull - ing me back - wards.

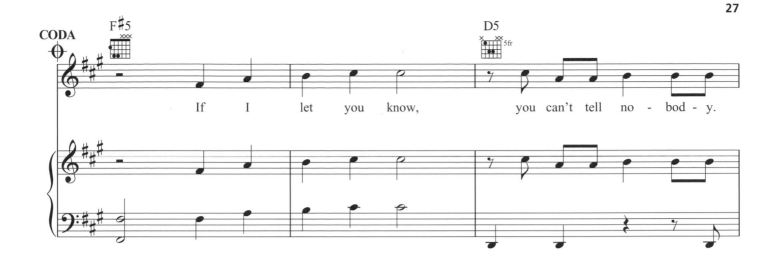

If I let you know, you can't tell no - bod - y.

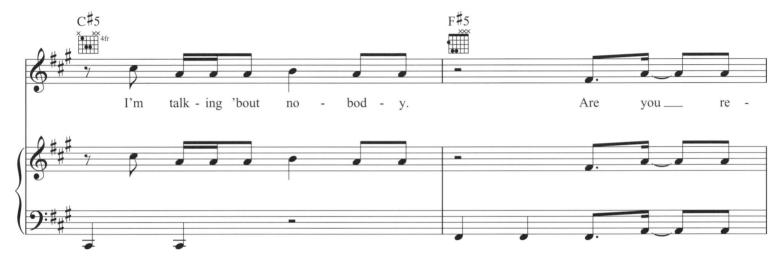

I'm talk - ing 'bout no - bod - y. Are you ___ re -

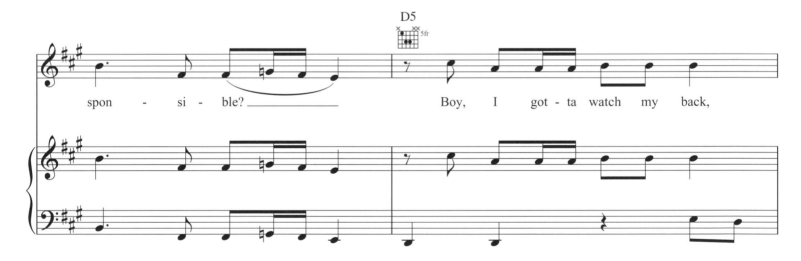

spon - si - ble? ___ Boy, I got - ta watch my back,

'cause I'm not just an - y - bod - y. "One: don't pick up the phone; ___ you

HAVANA

Words and Music by CAMILA CABELLO, LOUIS BELL,
PHARRELL WILLIAMS, ADAM FEENEY,
ALI TAMPOSI, BRIAN LEE,
ANDREW WOTMAN, BRITTANY HAZZARD,
JEFFERY LAMAR WILLIAMS and KAAN GUNESBERK

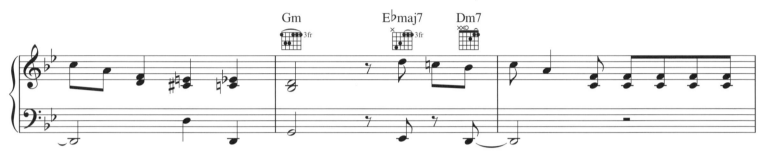

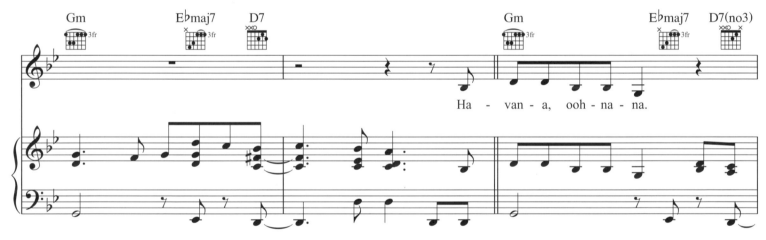

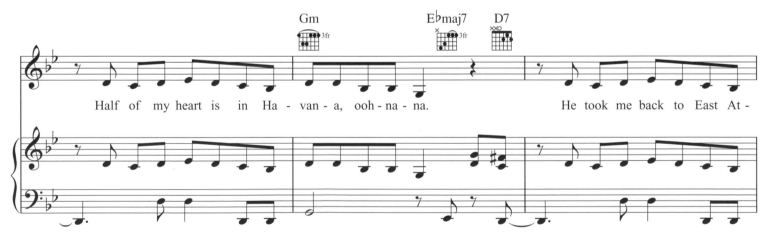

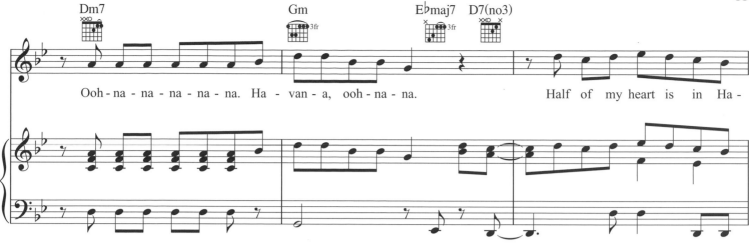

Ooh - na - na - na - na - na. Ha - van - a, ooh - na - na. Half of my heart is in Ha -

van - a, ooh - na - na. He took me back to East At - lan - ta, na - na - na.

Oh, but my heart is in Ha - van - a. My heart is in Ha - van - a, Ha - van - a, ooh - na -

na. Jef - fry just grad - u - at - ed, fresh on cam - pus, oh. _____ He's fresh out East At -

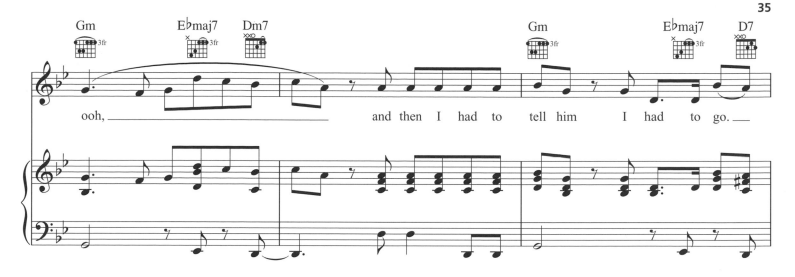

ooh, _____ and then I had to tell him I had to go. __

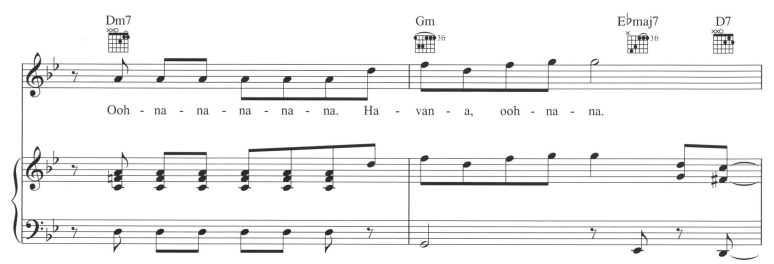

Ooh - na - na - na - na - na. Ha - van - a, ooh - na - na.

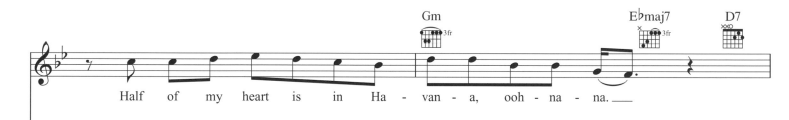

Half of my heart is in Ha - van - a, ooh - na - na. __

He took me back to East At - lan - ta, na - na - na.

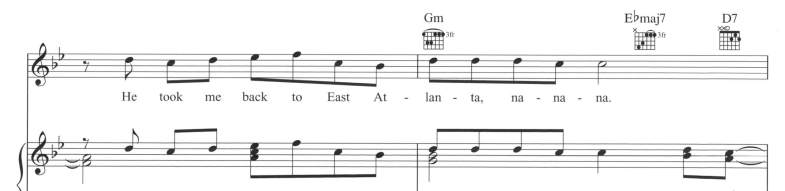

STAY

Words and Music by ALESSIA CARACCIOLO,
ANDERS FROEN, JONNALI PARMENIUS,
SARAH AARONS, ANTON ZASLAVSKI
and LINUS WIKLUND

Moderately, in 4

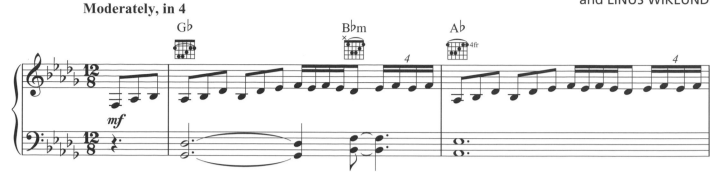

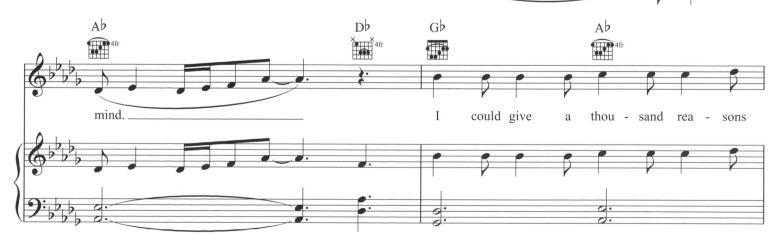

why. ___ Now I know ___ you, _ and you've got ___ to, ___ yeah. _

(♩. = ♩)

Make it on your own, but we don't have to grow up; we can stay for-ev-er young,

liv-ing on my so-fa, drink-ing rum and co-la un-der-neath the ris-ing sun.

I could give a thou-sand rea-sons why, but you're go-

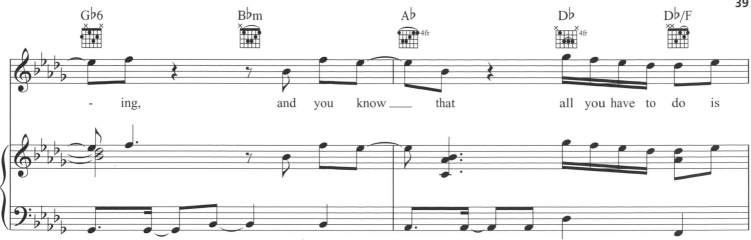

-ing, and you know ___ that all you have to do is

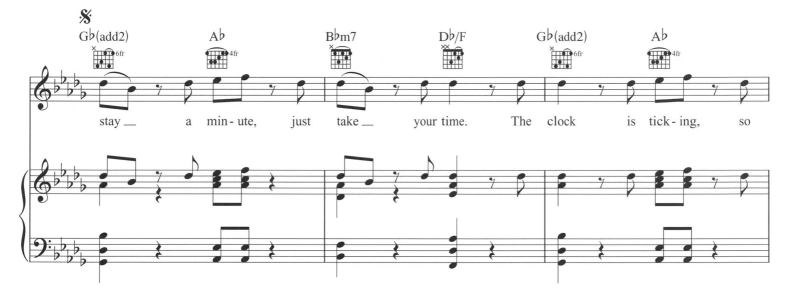

stay ___ a min- ute, just take ___ your time. The clock is tick- ing, so

stay. ___ All you have to do is wait ___ a sec- ond, your

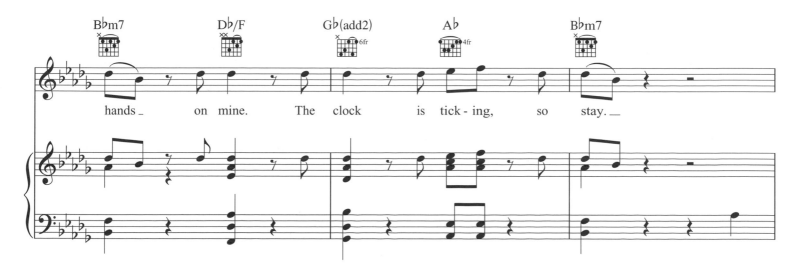

hands ___ on mine. The clock is tick- ing, so stay. ___

All ___ you have to ___ do ___ is
(All you have to do is,

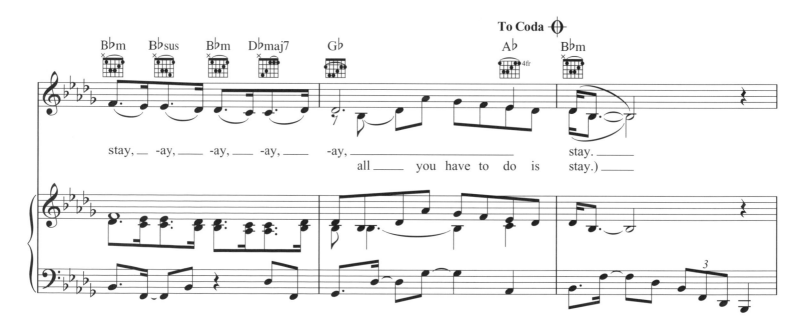

To Coda

stay, __ -ay, ___ -ay, ___ -ay, ___ -ay, _____ stay. ___
all ___ you have to do is stay.) ___

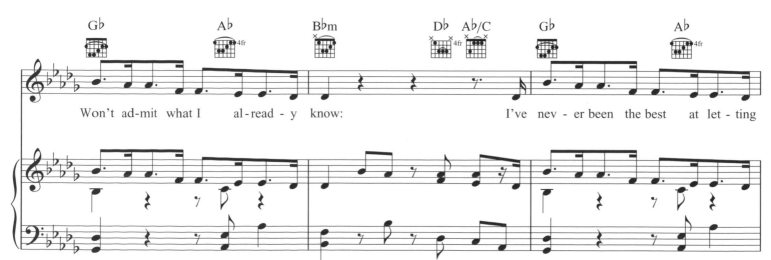

Won't ad-mit what I al-read-y know: I've nev-er been the best at let-ting

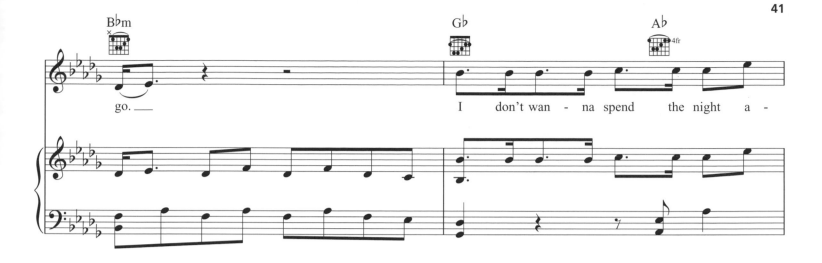

go. ___ I don't wan - na spend the night a -

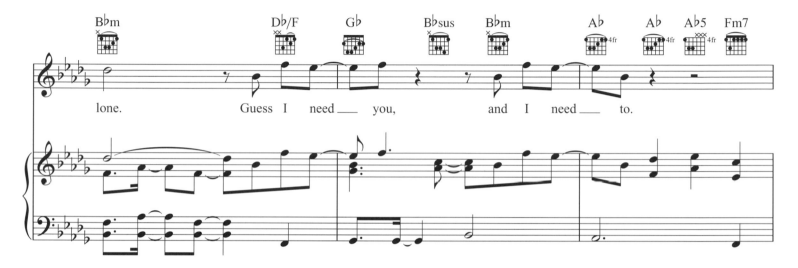

lone. Guess I need ___ you, and I need ___ to.

Make it on my own, but I don't wan-na grow up; we can stay for - ev - er young.

Liv-ing on my so - fa, drink-ing rum and co - la un-der-neath the ris - ing sun.

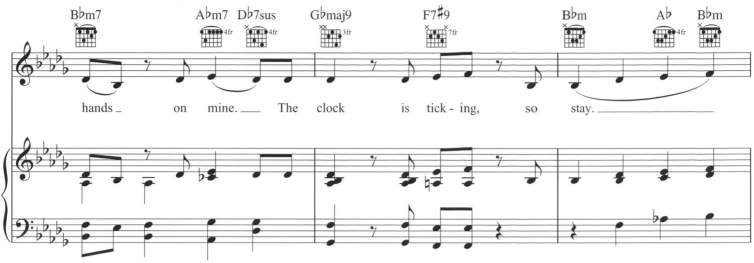

hands _ on mine. __ The clock is tick - ing, so stay. _____

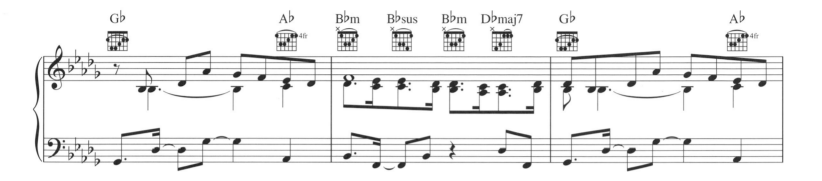

All _____ you have to ____ do _____ is
(All you have to do is,...)

stay, ___ -ay, ___ -ay, ___ -ay. ___ All ___ you have to do is stay. _____

PERFECT

Words and Music by
ED SHEERAN

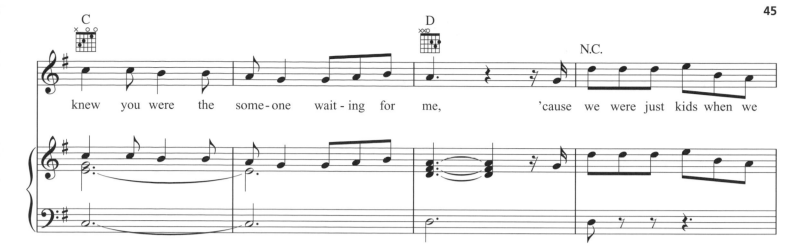

knew you were the some-one wait-ing for me, 'cause we were just kids when we

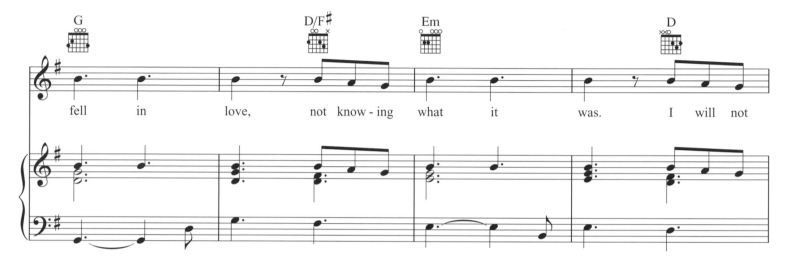

fell in love, not know-ing what it was. I will not

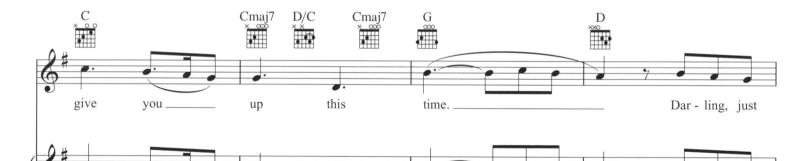

give you _____ up this time. _____ Dar - ling, just

kiss me slow. Your heart is all I own, and in your

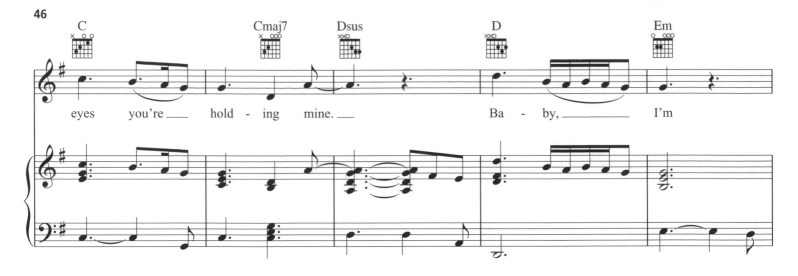

eyes you're ___ hold - ing mine. ___ Ba - by, ___ I'm

danc - ing in the dark with you be - tween my arms. Bare - foot on the

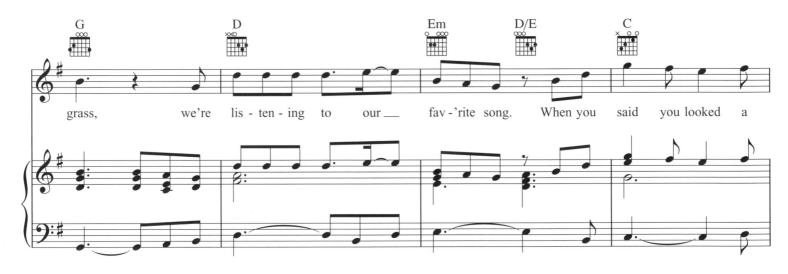

grass, we're lis - ten - ing to our ___ fav - 'rite song. When you said you looked a

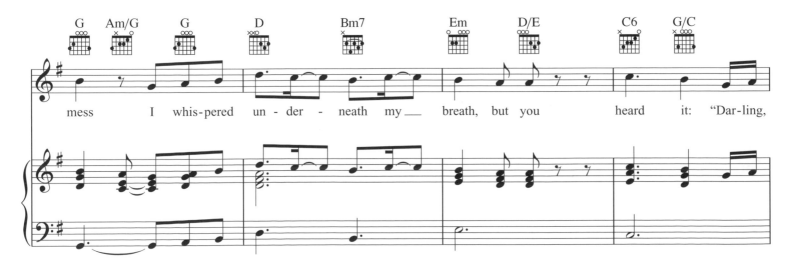

mess I whis - pered un - der - neath my ___ breath, but you heard it: "Dar - ling,

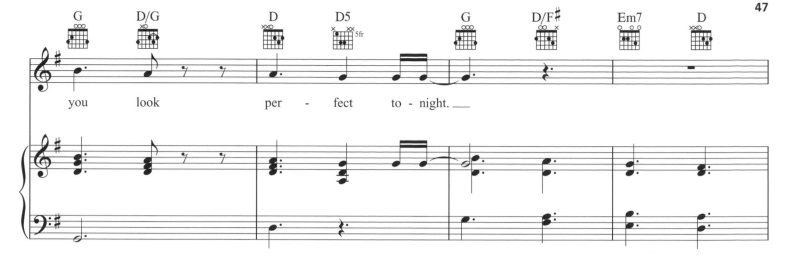

you look per - fect to - night. ___

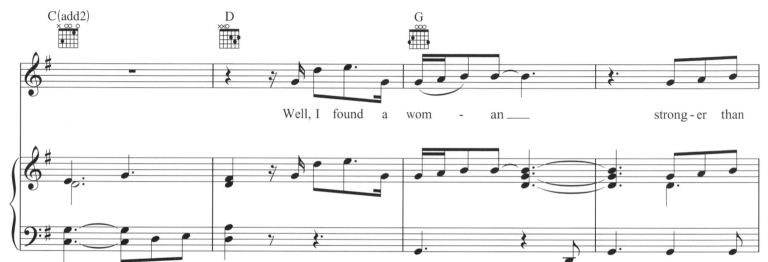

Well, I found a wom - an ___ strong - er than

an - y - one at all. She shares my dreams, I hope that some-day I'll share her

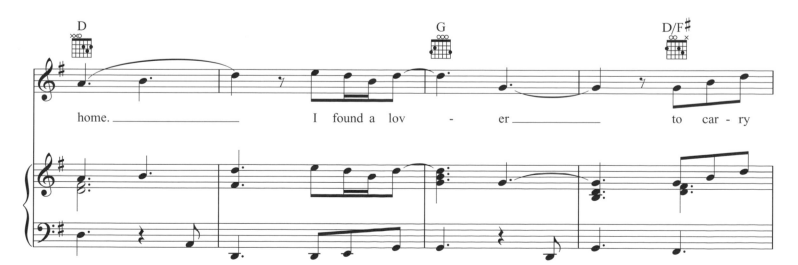

home. ___ I found a lov - er ___ to car - ry

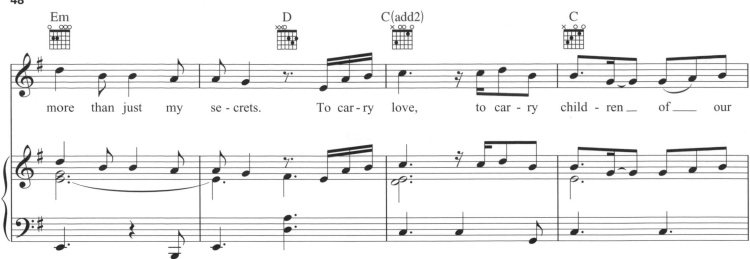

more than just my se - crets. To car - ry love, to car - ry child - ren __ of __ our

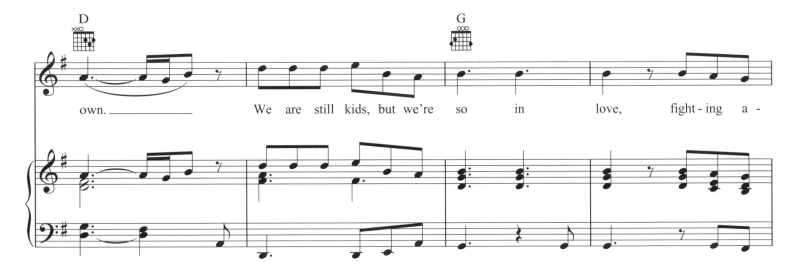

own. _____ We are still kids, but we're so in love, fight - ing a -

gainst all odds. I know we'll be al - right this

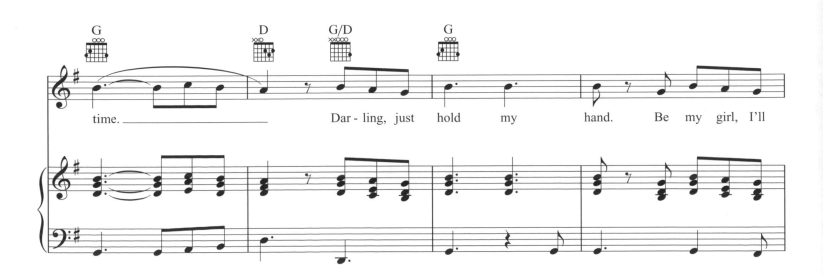

time. _____ Dar - ling, just hold my hand. Be my girl, I'll

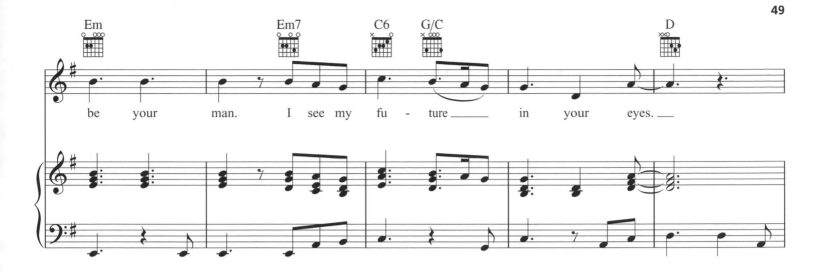

be your man. I see my fu - ture _____ in your eyes. ___

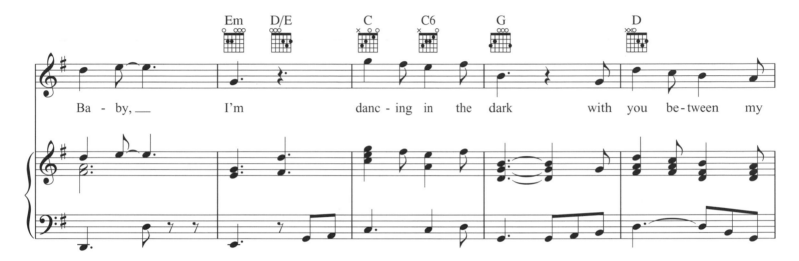

Ba - by, ___ I'm danc - ing in the dark with you be - tween my

arms. Bare - foot on the grass, we're lis - ten - ing to our ___

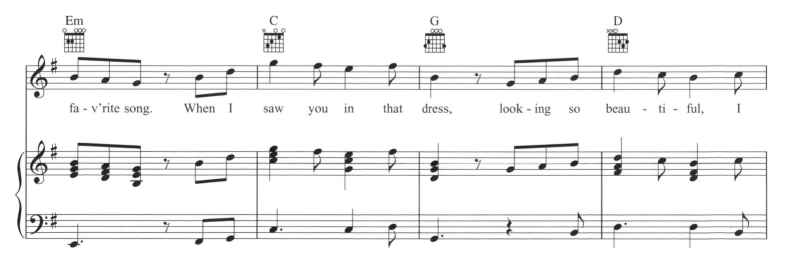

fa - v'rite song. When I saw you in that dress, look - ing so beau - ti - ful, I

don't de - serve it. Dar - ling, you look per - fect to - night. _

Cello solo ad lib.

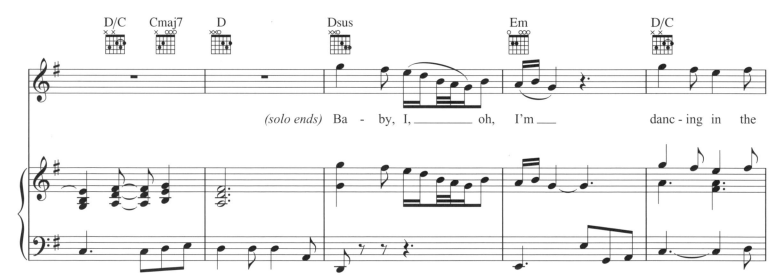

(solo ends) Ba - by, I, _____ oh, I'm ___ danc - ing in the

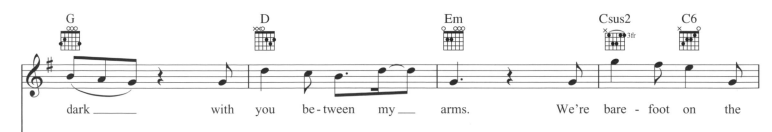

dark _____ with you be - tween my ___ arms. We're bare - foot on the

grass, _____ we're lis-ten-ing to our ___ fa-v'rite song. I have faith in what I

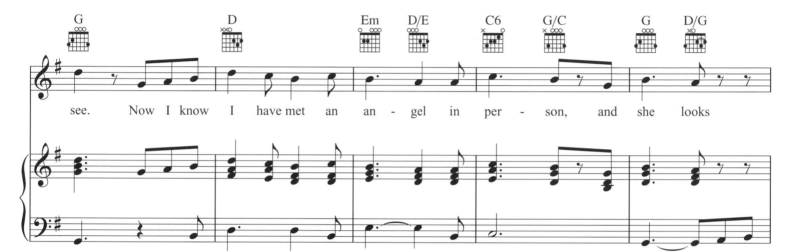

see. Now I know I have met an an-gel in per-son, and she looks

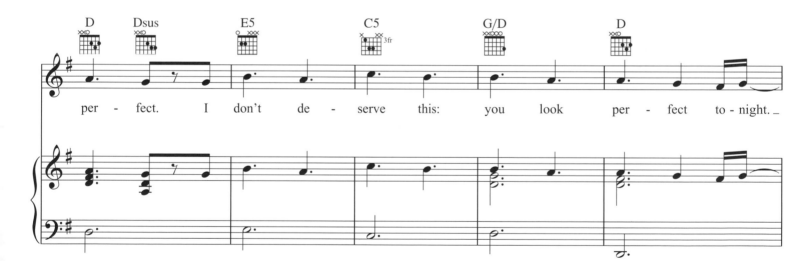

per-fect. I don't de-serve this: you look per-fect to-night. _

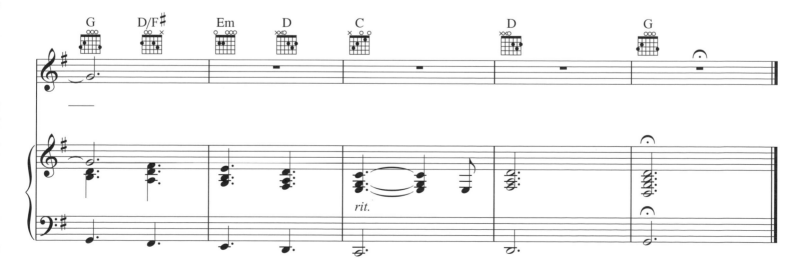

FEEL IT STILL

Words and Music by JOHN GOURLEY,
ZACH CAROTHERS, JASON SECHRIST,
ERIC HOWK, KYLE O'QUIN, BRIAN HOLLAND,
FREDDIE GORMAN, GEORGIA DOBBINS,
ROBERT BATEMAN, WILLIAM GARRETT,
JOHN HILL and ASA TACCONE

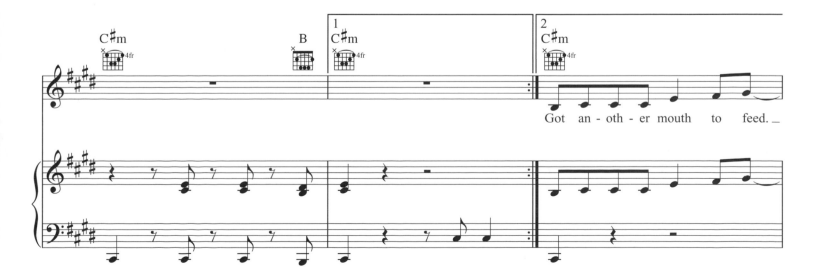

nine-teen six-ty six now. Might-a had your fill, but I feel it still

(but, -ut I feel __ it __ still). Ooh, _____ I'm a

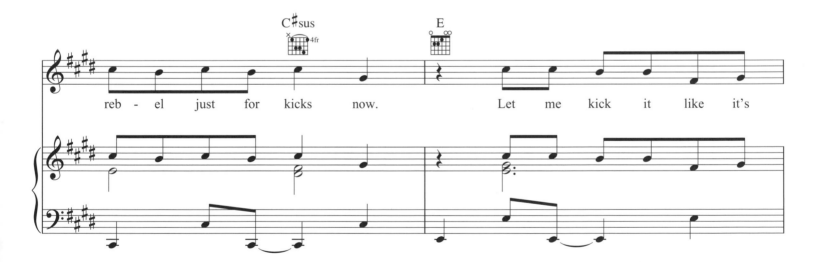

reb - el just for kicks now. Let me kick it like it's

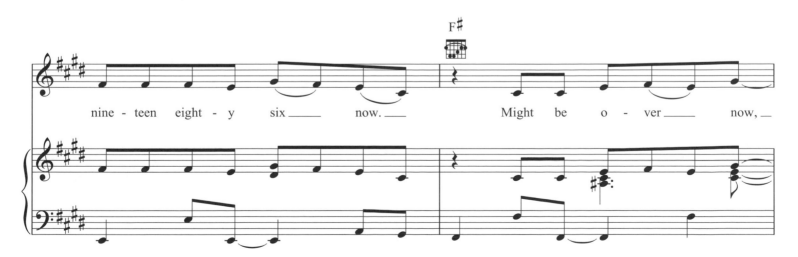

nine-teen eight-y six ___ now. ___ Might be o - ver ___ now, __

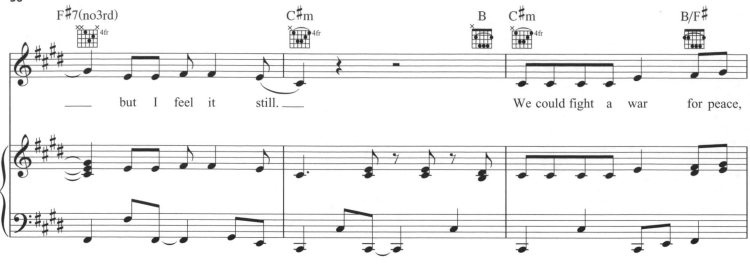

but I feel it still. ___ We could fight a war for peace,

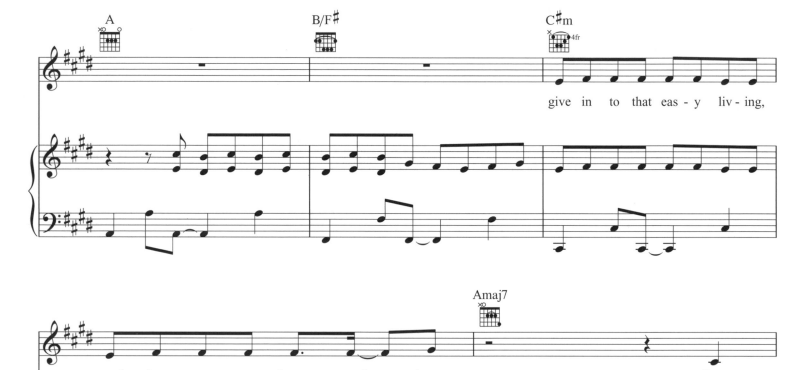

give in to that eas - y liv - ing,

good - bye to my hopes and ___ dreams. ___ Start

flip-ping for my en - e - mies. We could wait un - til the walls come down. ___

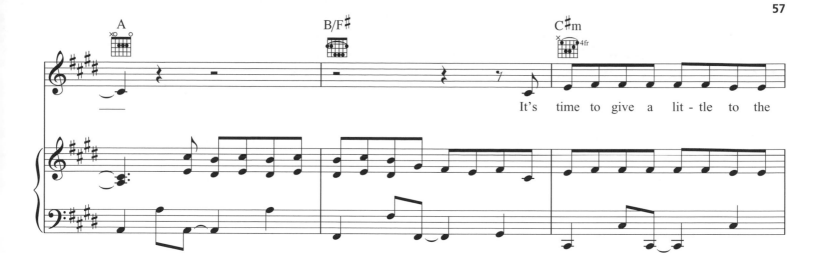

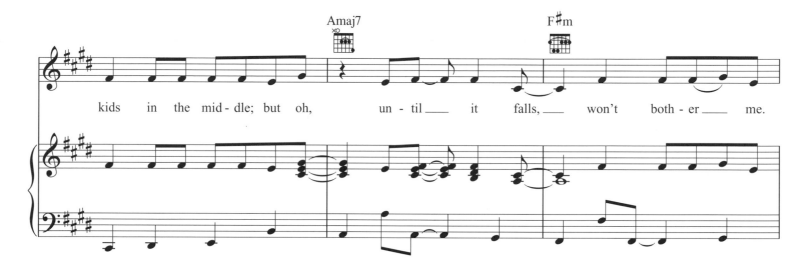

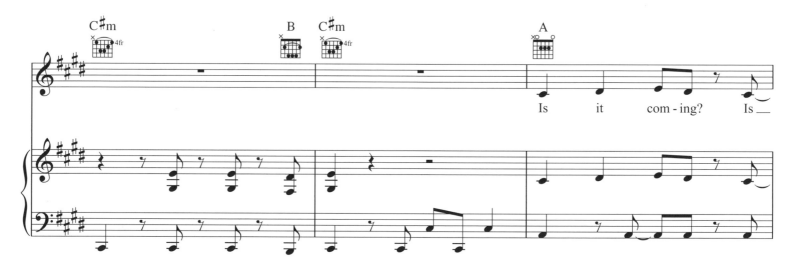

Might-a had your fill, _____ but I feel it still.

I've been do-ing it since nine-teen six-ty-six now.)

Is it com-ing? Is _____ it com-ing?

Might-a had your fill, but I feel it still.

(Might-a had your fill, but I feel it still.)

Might-a had your fill, but I feel it still.

Ooh, _____ I'm a

reb - el just for kicks. Yeah, your love is an a - byss for my

heart to e - clipse now. Might be o - ver ___ now, but I feel it still.

But I feel it, uh, uh, I feel it. Ooh, ___ I'm a

reb - el just for kicks now. I've been feel - ing it since nine-teen six - ty - six now.

Might be o - ver ___ now, but I feel it still.

Ooh, ___ I'm a reb - el just for kicks now.

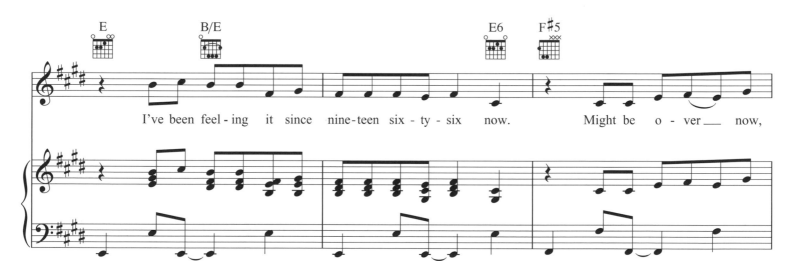

I've been feel - ing it since nine-teen six - ty - six now. Might be o - ver ___ now,

but I feel it still. Might-a had your fill, but I feel it still.

DESPACITO / SHAPE OF YOU

DESPACITO
Words and Music by LUIS FONSI,
ERIKA ENDER, JUSTIN BIEBER,
JASON BOYD, MARTY JAMES GARTON
and RAMON AYALA

SHAPE OF YOU
Words and Music by ED SHEERAN,
KEVIN BRIGGS, KANDI BURRUSS,
TAMEKA COTTLE, STEVE MAC
and JOHNNY McDAID

yeah. _____ Oh, __ whoa, you are _____ my sun-rise on a dark - est

day. Got me feel - ing some kind of way. Make me wan - na sa-vor ev-'ry mo-ment slow-

- ly, slow - ly, _____ yeah. Tú, tú e - res el i - mán y yo soy __ el me -

tal. Me voy a-cer-can-do voy ar - man-do el plan. Só - lo con pen-sar-lo se a __ ce-la-ra el

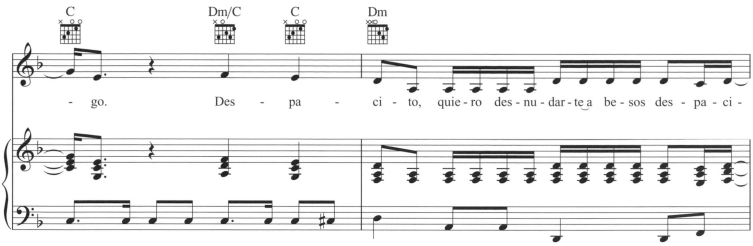

-go. Des - pa - ci - to, quie-ro des-nu-dar-te a be-sos des - pa - ci -

- to, fir-mo en las pa-re-des de tu___ la-ber-in - to. Y ha-cer de tu cuer-po to-do un ma - nu scri -

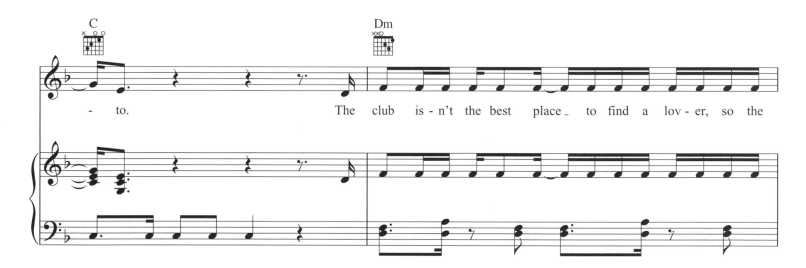

- to. The club is-n't the best place___ to find a lov - er, so the

bar is where I go.___ Me and my friends___ at the ta - ble do-ing shots, drink-ing

C   Dm   Dm7

I may be cra-zy; don't mind me, say: Boy, ya no ha-blem-os no,

Bb   F

to-ma mi cuer-po y fró-ta-lo con-tra___ ti. Ven y si-gue has-ta el fin, ven,

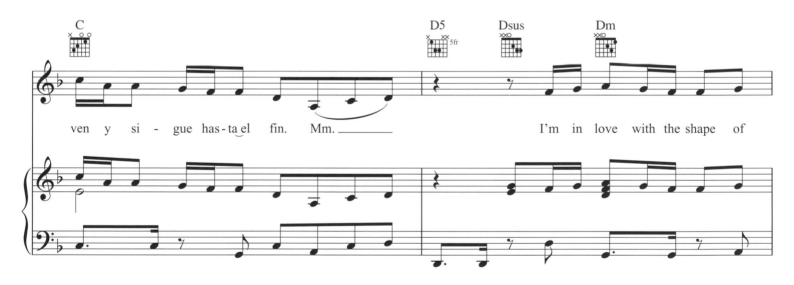

C   D5   Dsus   Dm

ven y si-gue has-ta el fin. Mm._____ I'm in love with the shape of

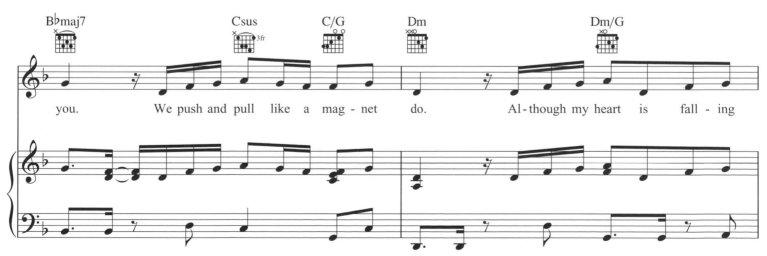

Bbmaj7   Csus   C/G   Dm   Dm/G

you. We push and pull like a mag-net do. Al-though my heart is fall-ing

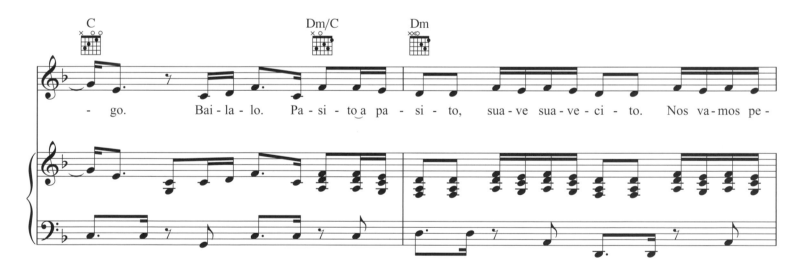

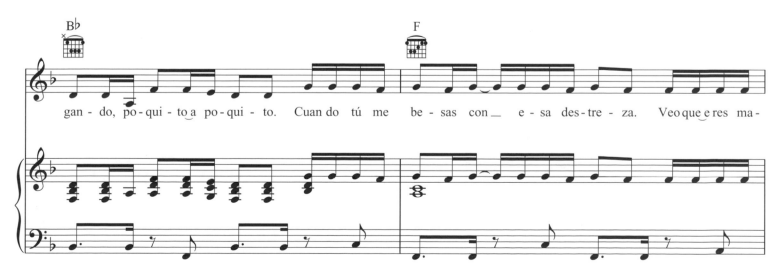

room, and now my bed-sheets smell like you. Ev-'ry day dis-cov-er-ing some-thing brand

Bai - la - lo.   Des - pa - ci - to.   Oh. _____

new.   I'm in love with your bod - y.   Oh I, oh I, oh I, oh I, mm.

_____   Des - pa -

Oh I, oh I, oh I, oh I, ah

Come on, ___ be my ba - by.

ci - to.

Oh yeah.

PRAYING

Words and Music by KESHA SEBERT,
BEN ABRAHAM, RYAN LEWIS
and ANDREW JOSLYN

breathe a-gain. ___ And you said that I ___ was done,

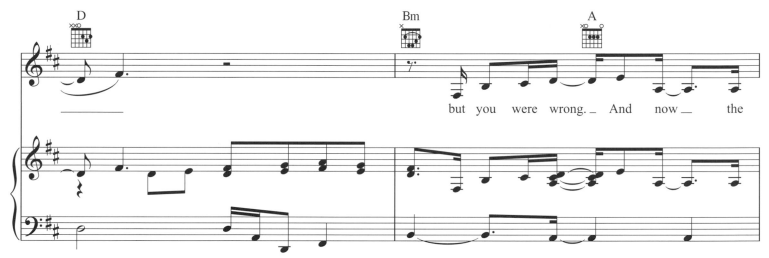

___ but you were wrong. ___ And now ___ the

best is yet ___ to come. _____ I can make it on ___ my own. ___

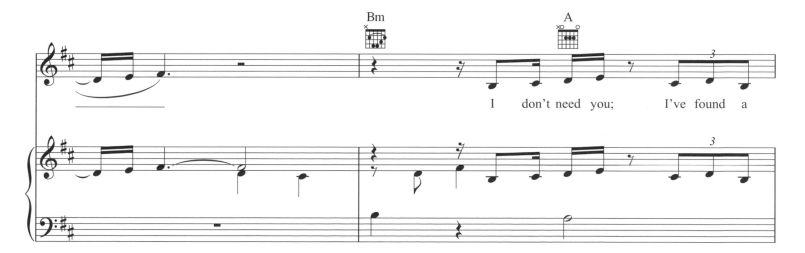

_____ I don't need you; I've found a

I'll just say this: it's, "I wish you well." _____ I hope you're some-where pray - ing, __

__ pray - ing. I hope your soul is chang - ing, __

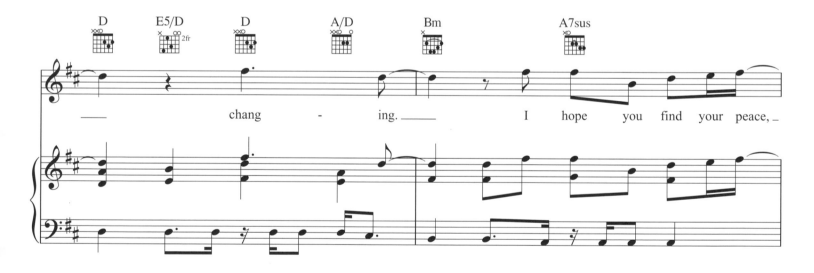

__ chang - ing. ____ I hope you find your peace, __

__ fall - ing on ___ your knees, ___ pray - ing. __

SORRY NOT SORRY

Words and Music by DEMITRIA LOVATO,
SEAN DOUGLAS, WARREN FELDER,
WILLIAM SIMMONS and TREVOR BROWN

Moderately slow

Now I'm out here look-ing like re-venge, feel-ing like a

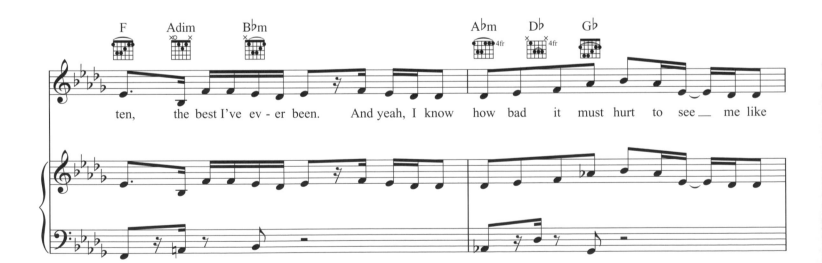

ten, the best I've ev-er been. And yeah, I know how bad it must hurt to see ___ me like

'cause the ta-bles have turned. _ Yeah, I'm on fire, _ and I know that it burns. _

Talk that talk, ba-by. Bet-ter walk, bet-ter walk that walk, ba-by. If you talk, if you

talk that talk, _ ba-by, bet-ter walk, bet-ter walk that walk, ba-by.

ISSUES

Words and Music by BENJAMIN LEVIN,
MIKKEL ERIKSEN, TOR HERMANSEN,
JULIA MICHAELS and JUSTIN TRANTER

Moderately, in 2

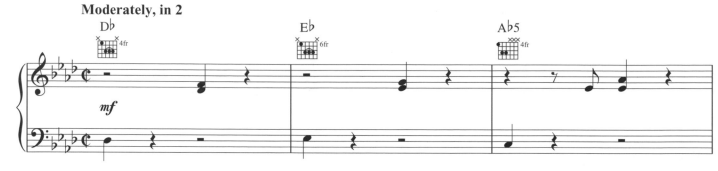

I'm jeal-ous; I'm o-ver-zeal-ous: when I'm

down I get real down; when I'm high I don't come down. But I get

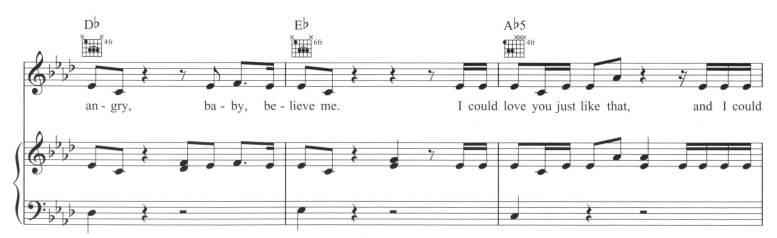

an-gry, ba-by, be-lieve me. I could love you just like that, and I could

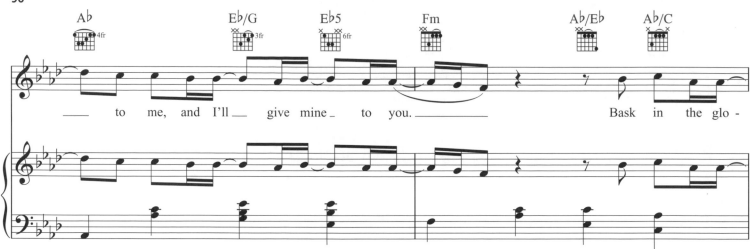

to me, and I'll ___ give mine ___ to you. ___ Bask in the glo-

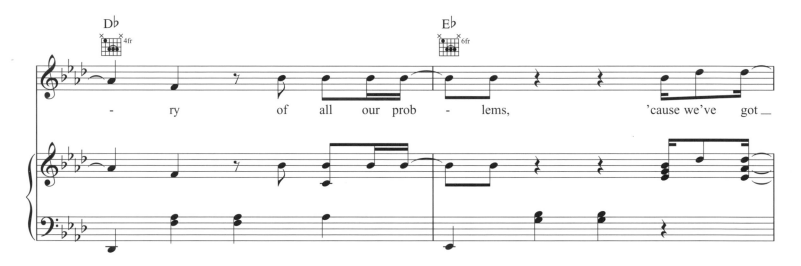

-ry of all our prob-lems, 'cause we've got ___

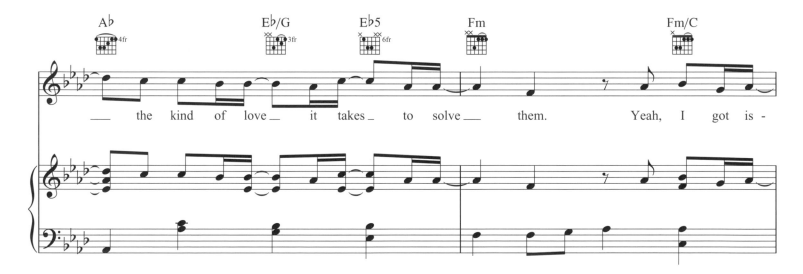

___ the kind of love ___ it takes ___ to solve ___ them. Yeah, I got is-

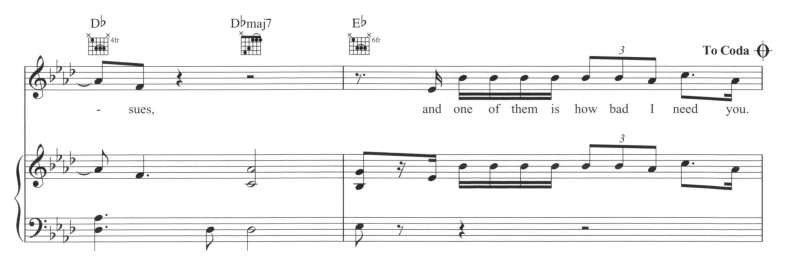

-sues, and one of them is how bad I need you.

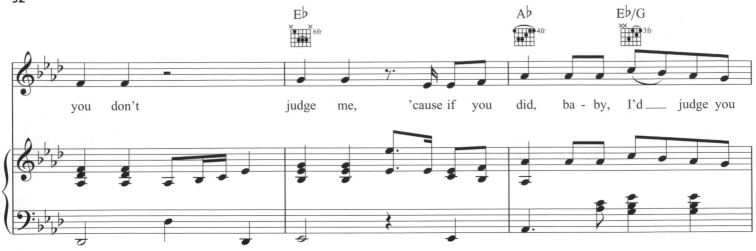

you don't judge me, 'cause if you did, ba - by, I'd___ judge you

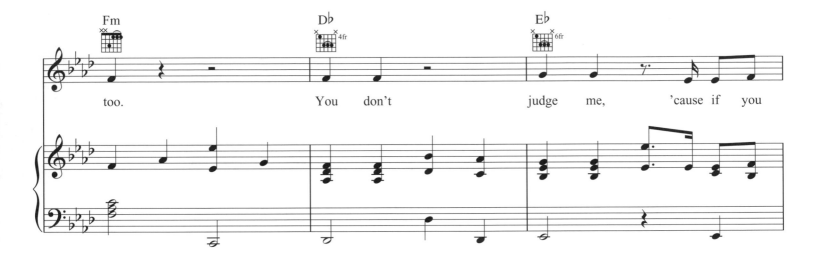

too. You don't judge me, 'cause if you

D.S. al Coda

did, ba - by, I'd___ judge you too. 'Cause I got is -

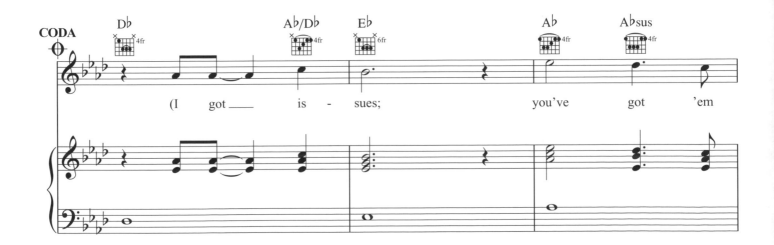

CODA

(I got ___ is - sues; you've got 'em

too.) Well, one of them is how bad I need you. (I got ___ is - sues;

you've got 'em too.) _____ 'Cause I got is - sues. You've got 'em

too. So give them all ___ to me, and I'll ___ give mine _ to you. _

_____ Bask in the glo - ry of all our prob - lems, 'cause we've got _

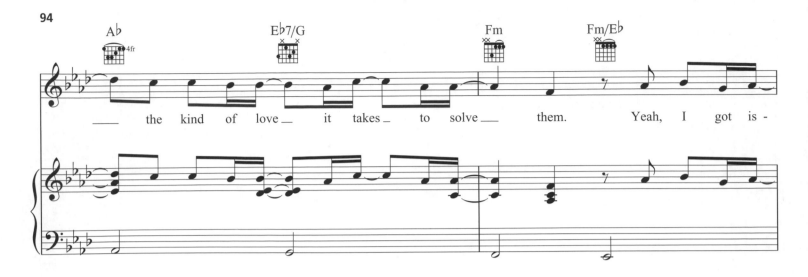

the kind of love ___ it takes ___ to solve ___ them. Yeah, I got is -

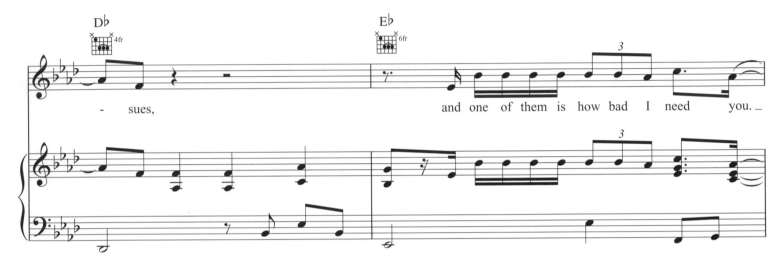

- sues, and one of them is how bad I need you. ___

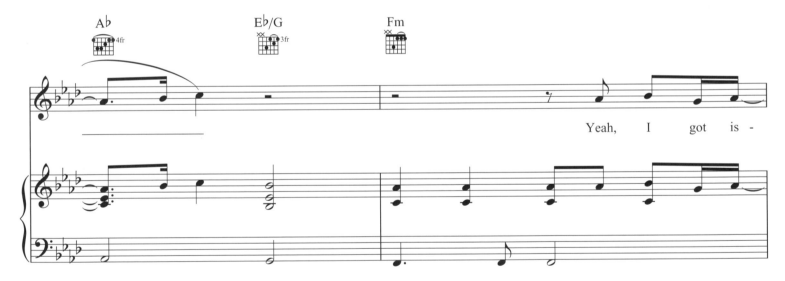

_____ Yeah, I got is -

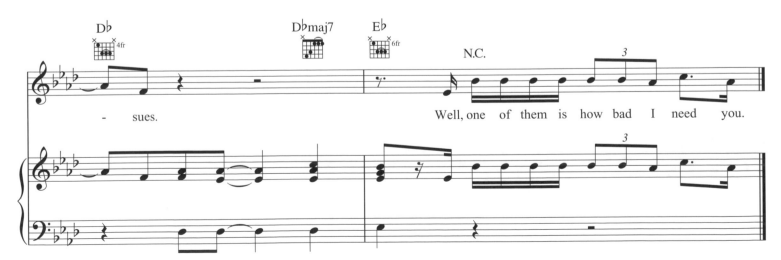

- sues. Well, one of them is how bad I need you.

BETTER THAN KARAOKE!

Whether you're a karaoke singer or an auditioning professional, the **Pro Vocal®** series is for you! Unlike most karaoke packs, each book in the Pro Vocal series contains the lyrics, melody, and chord symbols for at least eight hit songs. The audio contains demos for listening, and separate backing tracks so you can sing along. Perfect for home rehearsal, parties, auditions, corporate events, and gigs without a backup band.

WOMEN'S EDITIONS

00740247	**1. Broadway Songs**	$14.95
00740249	**2. Jazz Standards**	$16.99
00740246	**3. Contemporary Hits**	$14.95
00740277	**4. '80s Gold**	$12.95
00740279	**7. R&B Super Hits**	$12.95
00740309	**8. Wedding Gems**	$12.95
00740344	**11. Disney's Best**	$16.99
00740378	**12. Ella Fitzgerald**	$14.95
00740350	**14. Musicals of Boublil & Schönberg**	$14.95
00740342	**16. Disney Favorites**	$15.99
00740353	**17. Jazz Ballads**	$14.99
00740376	**18. Jazz Vocal Standards**	$17.99
00740354	**21. Jazz Favorites**	$14.99
00740374	**22. Patsy Cline**	$14.95
00740369	**23. Grease**	$14.95
00740367	**25. Mamma Mia**	$15.99
00740365	**26. Movie Songs**	$14.95
00740363	**29. Torch Songs**	$14.95
00740379	**30. Hairspray**	$15.99
00740388	**33. Billie Holiday**	$14.95
00740390	**35. Contemporary Christian**	$14.95
00740392	**36. Wicked**	$17.99
00740396	**39. Christmas Hits**	$15.95
00740419	**45. Sing Broadway**	$14.99
00740420	**46. More Standards**	$14.99
00740421	**47. Timeless Hits**	$14.99
00740422	**48. Easygoing R&B**	$14.99
00740426	**51. Great Standards Collection**	$19.99
00740430	**52. Worship Favorites**	$14.99
00740434	**53. Lullabyes**	$14.99
00740444	**55. Amy Winehouse**	$15.99
00160119	**56. Adele**	$16.99
00740446	**57. The Grammy Awards Best Female Pop Vocal Performance 1990-1999**	$14.99
00740447	**58. The Grammy Awards Best Female Pop Vocal Performance 2000-2009**	$14.99
00109374	**60. Katy Perry**	$14.99
00123120	**62. Top Downloads**	$14.99

MEN'S EDITIONS

00740250	**2. Jazz Standards**	$14.95
00740298	**5. Christmas Standards**	$15.95
00740280	**6. R&B Super Hits**	$12.95
00740411	**9. Broadway Greats**	$14.99
00740333	**10. Elvis Presley – Volume 1**	$14.95
00740347	**13. Frank Sinatra Classics**	$14.95
00740334	**14. Lennon & McCartney**	$14.99
00740453	**15. Queen**	$14.99
00740335	**16. Elvis Presley – Volume 2**	$14.99
00740351	**18. Musicals of Boublil & Schönberg**	$14.95
00740337	**19. Lennon & McCartney – Volume 2**	$14.99
00740346	**20. Frank Sinatra Standards**	$14.95
00740338	**21. Lennon & McCartney – Volume 3**	$14.99
00740358	**22. Great Standards**	$14.99
00740336	**23. Elvis Presley**	$14.99
00740341	**24. Duke Ellington**	$14.99
00740339	**25. Lennon & McCartney – Volume 4**	$14.99
00740359	**26. Pop Standards**	$14.99
00740362	**27. Michael Bublé**	$15.99
00740454	**28. Maroon 5**	$14.99
00740364	**29. Torch Songs**	$14.95
00740366	**30. Movie Songs**	$14.95

00740368	**31. Hip Hop Hits**	$14.95
00740370	**32. Grease**	$14.95
00740371	**33. Josh Groban**	$14.95
00740373	**34. Billy Joel**	$14.99
00740382	**36. Hits of the '60s**	$14.95
00740385	**38. Motown**	$14.95
00740386	**39. Hank Williams**	$14.95
00740387	**40. Neil Diamond**	$14.95
00740391	**41. Contemporary Christian**	$14.95
00740399	**43. Ray**	$14.95
00740400	**44. The Rat Pack Hits**	$14.99
00740401	**45. Songs in the Style of Nat "King" Cole**	$14.99
00740402	**46. At the Lounge**	$14.95
00740403	**47. The Big Band Singer**	$14.95
00740427	**52. Great Standards Collection**	$19.99
00740431	**53. Worship Favorites**	$14.99
00740435	**54. Barry Manilow**	$14.99
00740436	**55. Lionel Richie**	$14.99
00740439	**56. Michael Bublé – Crazy Love**	$15.99
00740441	**57. Johnny Cash**	$14.99
00148089	**58. Bruno Mars**	$15.99
00740448	**59. The Grammy Awards Best Male Pop Vocal Performance 1990-1999**	$14.99
00740449	**60. The Grammy Awards Best Male Pop Vocal Performance 2000-2009**	$14.99
00740452	**61. Michael Bublé – Call Me Irresponsible**	$14.99
00101777	**62. Michael Bublé – Christmas**	$19.99
00137717	**63. Jersey Boys**	$14.99
00123119	**65. Top Downloads**	$14.99

EXERCISES

00123770	**Vocal Exercises**	$14.99
00740395	**Vocal Warm-Ups**	$14.99

MIXED EDITIONS

These editions feature songs for both male and female voices.

00740311	**1. Wedding Duets**	$12.95
00740398	**2. Enchanted**	$14.95
00740407	**3. Rent**	$14.95
00740408	**4. Broadway Favorites**	$14.99
00740413	**5. South Pacific**	$15.99
00740429	**7. Christmas Carols**	$14.99
00740437	**8. Glee**	$16.99
00116960	**11. Les Misérables**	$19.99
00126476	**12. Frozen**	$16.99

KIDS EDITIONS

00740451 **1. Songs Children Can Sing!** .. $14.99

Visit Hal Leonard online at
www.halleonard.com

Prices, contents, & availability
subject to change without notice.

Disney characters and artwork
© Disney Enterprises, Inc.

0718